CSS Box Model

Abdelfattah Ragab

CSS Box Model and Layouts

Abdelfattah Ragab

Introduction

Welcome to the book "CSS Box Model and Layouts".
In this book, I explain the properties of CSS box model
such as width, height, margin, padding and so on.
By the end of this book, you will be able to position your
box correctly on the page, control its size and spacing,
and handle all kinds of scenarios.
Let us go!

Chapter 1: Understanding the box model

The CSS3 box model is a fundamental concept that describes how elements are rendered and how their size and spacing are calculated in CSS. It consists of four layers or components: content, padding, border, and margin. Understanding the box model is crucial for controlling the layout and spacing of elements on a web page. Let's explore each component in detail:

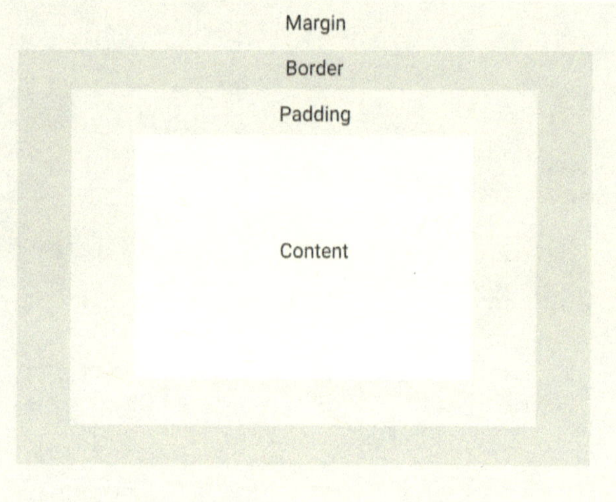

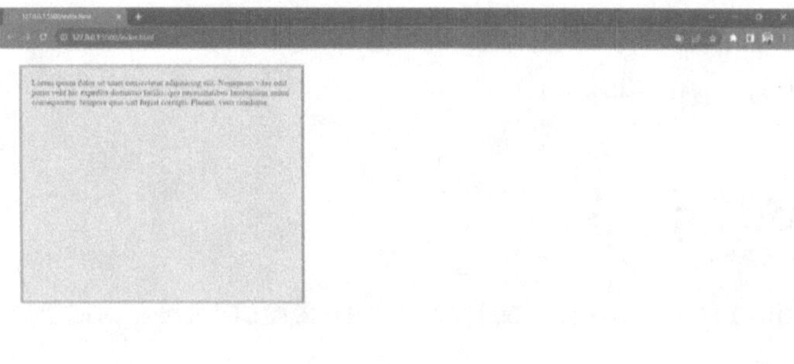

Open browser inspect - dev tools

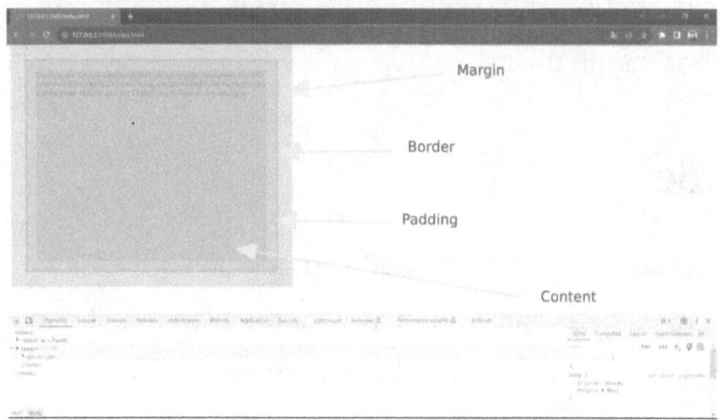

Content

The content area represents the actual content or text inside an element. It has a width and height that can be explicitly set using CSS properties like width and height.

By default, the content area does not include padding, border, or margin.

Padding

Padding is the space between the content area and the element's border. It helps create space around the content without affecting the element's overall size. Padding can be set using properties like padding-top, padding-right, padding-bottom, and padding-left. The padding value can be specified in pixels, percentages, or other length units.

Border

The border surrounds the padding and content areas and provides a visible boundary for the element. It can be styled using properties like border-width, border-style, and border-color. Borders can have different styles such as solid, dotted, dashed, or none. The border width can be set independently for each side using properties like border-top-width, border-right-width, border-bottom-width, and border-left-width.

Margin

The margin is the space outside the element, creating separation between neighboring elements. It helps control the spacing between elements on a webpage. Margins can be set using properties like margin-top, margin-right, margin-bottom, and margin-left. Like padding, margin values can be specified in pixels, percentages, or other length units.

Chapter 2: Understanding Box Sizing

By default, the width and height properties of an element control only the content area. However, the CSS property box-sizing allows you to change this behavior. By setting box-sizing: border-box;, the width and height properties include both the content and padding areas, making it easier to calculate the overall size of an element.

Calculating Total Width and Height

To determine the total width and height of an element, you need to consider the content width/height, padding, border, and margin. The total width is calculated as follows:

> Total Width = content width + left padding + right padding + left border + right border + left margin + right margin

The total height is calculated similarly, taking into account the top and bottom padding, border, and margin.

box-sizing

The box-sizing CSS property sets how the total width and height of an element is calculated.
It allows us to include the padding and border in an element's total width and height.

By default, the width and height of an element are calculated as follows:

> width + padding + border = actual width of an element height + padding + border = actual height of an element

This means: If you specify the width/height of an element, the element often appears larger than you have specified (because the border and padding of the element are added to the specified width/height of the element).

Values

- content-box (default)
- border-box

Here are two div elements that are identical and differ only in the value of the box-sizing property

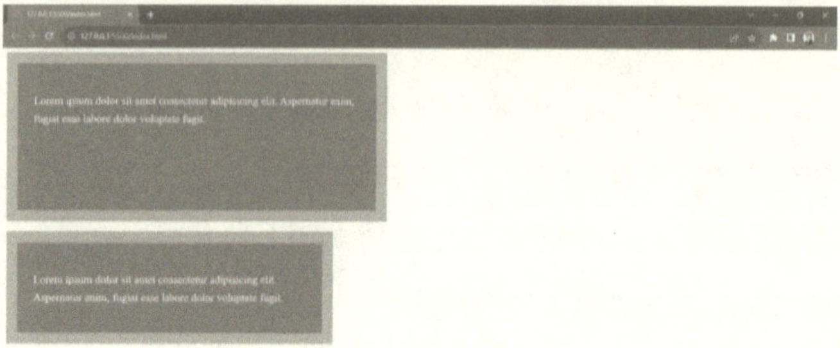

```css
<style>
  .box {
    width: 600px;
    height: 200px;
    padding: 30px;
    color: white;
    font-size: 20px;
    line-height: 1.6em;
    background-color: rgb(0, 100, 128);
    border: 20px solid rgb(252, 49, 232);
  }
  .box-1 {
    box-sizing: content-box;
  }
  .box-2 {
    box-sizing: border-box;
  }
```

```html
</style>
<div class="box box-1">
  <p>
    Lorem ipsum dolor sit amet consectetur
adipisicing elit. Aspernatur enim,
    fugiat esse labore dolor voluptate fugit.
  </p>
</div>
<br />
<div class="box box-2">
  <p>
    Lorem ipsum dolor sit amet consectetur
adipisicing elit. Aspernatur enim,
    fugiat esse labore dolor voluptate fugit.
  </p>
</div>
```

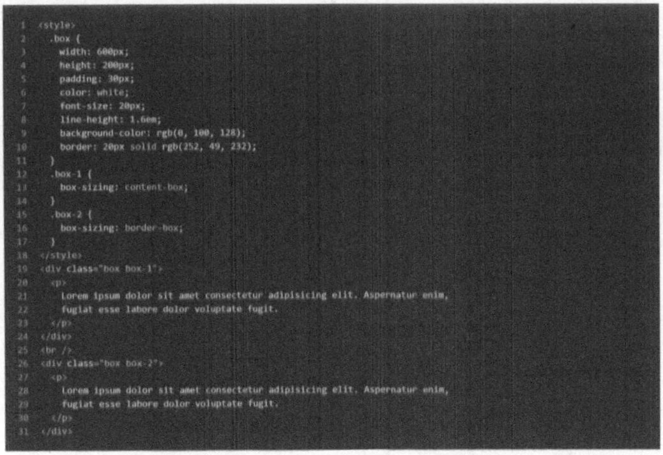

```
1   <style>
2     .box {
3       width: 600px;
4       height: 200px;
5       padding: 30px;
6       color: white;
7       font-size: 20px;
8       line-height: 1.6em;
9       background-color: rgb(0, 100, 128);
10      border: 20px solid rgb(252, 49, 232);
11    }
12    .box-1 {
13      box-sizing: content-box;
14    }
15    .box-2 {
16      box-sizing: border-box;
17    }
18  </style>
19  <div class="box box-1">
20    <p>
21      Lorem ipsum dolor sit amet consectetur adipisicing elit. Aspernatur enim,
22      fugiat esse labore dolor voluptate fugit.
23    </p>
24  </div>
25  <br />
26  <div class="box box-2">
27    <p>
28      Lorem ipsum dolor sit amet consectetur adipisicing elit. Aspernatur enim,
29      fugiat esse labore dolor voluptate fugit.
30    </p>
31  </div>
```

content-box (default)

The content-box value represents the traditional box model. With content-box, the width and height of an element are calculated by considering only the content area and excluding padding and border. In other words: If you add padding or a border to the element, its overall width and height will increase.

For example:

```
<style>
  .box {
    width: 600px;
    height: 200px;
    padding: 30px;
    color: white;
    font-size: 20px;
    line-height: 1.6em;
```

```
    background-color: rgb(0, 100, 128);
    border: 20px solid rgb(252, 49, 232);
    box-sizing: content-box;
  }
</style>
<div class="box">
  <p>
    Lorem ipsum dolor sit amet consectetur
adipisicing elit. Aspernatur enim,
    fugiat esse labore dolor voluptate fugit.
  </p>
</div>
```

```
1   <style>
2     .box {
3       width: 600px;
4       height: 200px;
5       padding: 30px;
6       color: white;
7       font-size: 20px;
8       line-height: 1.6em;
9       background-color: rgb(0, 100, 128);
10      border: 20px solid rgb(252, 49, 232);
11      box-sizing: content-box;
12    }
13  </style>
14  <div class="box">
15    <p>
16      Lorem ipsum dolor sit amet consectetur adipisicing elit. Aspernatur enim,
17      fugiat esse labore dolor voluptate fugit.
18    </p>
19  </div>
```

border-box

The box-sizing property allows us to include padding and margins in the overall width and height of an element.

If you set box-sizing: border-box; on an element, padding and border are included in the width and height:

```
.box {
  width: 600px;
  height: 200px;
  padding: 30px;
  color: white;
  font-size: 20px;
  line-height: 1.6em;
  background-color: rgb(0, 100, 128);
  border: 20px solid rgb(252, 49, 232);
  box-sizing: border-box;
}
```

```
.box {
  width: 600px;
  height: 200px;
  padding: 30px;
  color: white;
  font-size: 20px;
  line-height: 1.6em;
  background-color: rgb(0, 100, 128);
  border: 20px solid rgb(252, 49, 232);
  box-sizing: border-box;
}
```

The total size of the element remains 600 pixels by 200 pixels, and the padding and border are included within this size.

In summary, the box-sizing property allows you to control how the total width and height of an element are calculated, providing flexibility in handling padding and border sizes.
Understanding and utilizing the CSS3 box model is essential for creating well-structured, visually appealing layouts. By manipulating the content, padding, border, and margin properties, you can control the dimensions and spacing of elements on your web page precisely.

Chapter 3: Margin and Padding Properties

margin

The CSS margin properties are used to create space around elements, outside of any defined borders.

This property can have between one and four values:

- margin: <top> <right> <bottom> <left>
- margin: <top> <right and left> <bottom>
- margin: <top and bottom> <right and left>
- margin: <all sides>

Values

- length
- percentage
- auto

We have two div elements

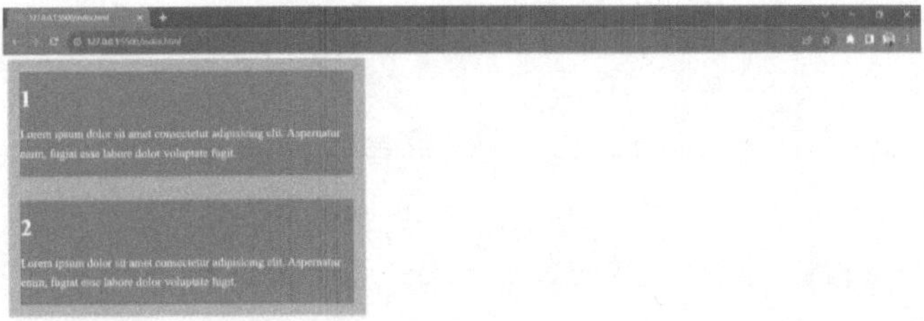

```
<style>
  .box {
    width: 600px;
    height: auto;
    color: white;
    font-size: 20px;
    line-height: 1.6em;
    background-color: rgb(0, 100, 128);
    border: 20px solid rgb(252, 49, 232);
    box-sizing: border-box;
  }
  .box-1 {
  }
  .box-2 {
  }
</style>
<div class="box box-1">
```

```
  <h1>1</h1>
  <p>
    Lorem ipsum dolor sit amet consectetur
adipisicing elit. Aspernatur enim,
    fugiat esse labore dolor voluptate fugit.
  </p>
</div>
<div class="box box-2">
  <h1>2</h1>
  <p>
    Lorem ipsum dolor sit amet consectetur
adipisicing elit. Aspernatur enim,
    fugiat esse labore dolor voluptate fugit.
  </p>
</div>
```

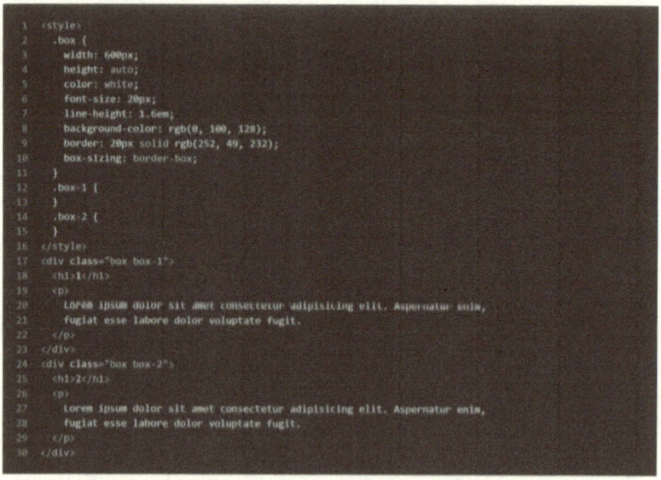

```
 1  <style>
 2    .box {
 3      width: 600px;
 4      height: auto;
 5      color: white;
 6      font-size: 20px;
 7      line-height: 1.6em;
 8      background-color: rgb(0, 100, 128);
 9      border: 20px solid rgb(252, 49, 232);
10      box-sizing: border-box;
11    }
12    .box-1 {
13    }
14    .box-2 {
15    }
16  </style>
17  <div class="box box-1">
18    <h1>1</h1>
19    <p>
20      Lorem ipsum dolor sit amet consectetur adipisicing elit. Aspernatur enim,
21      fugiat esse labore dolor voluptate fugit.
22    </p>
23  </div>
24  <div class="box box-2">
25    <h1>2</h1>
26    <p>
27      Lorem ipsum dolor sit amet consectetur adipisicing elit. Aspernatur enim,
28      fugiat esse labore dolor voluptate fugit.
29    </p>
30  </div>
```

We want to give space around the first element using the margin property

length

The size of the margin as a fixed value.

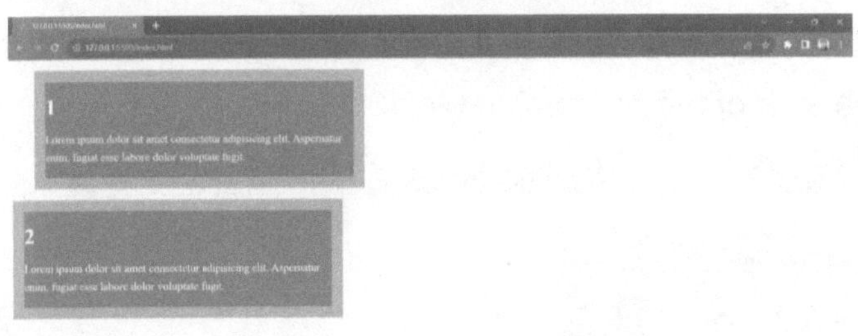

```
.box-1 {

    margin-top: 20px;

    margin-right: 40px;

    margin-bottom: 20px;

    margin-left: 40px;

}
```

```
12    .box-1 {
13      margin-top: 20px;
14      margin-right: 40px;
15      margin-bottom: 20px;
16      margin-left: 40px;
17    }
```

You can use the shorthand property as follows

```
.box-1 {

    margin: 20px 40px 20px 40px;
```

```css
}
```

```
12   .box-1 {
13     margin: 20px 40px 20px 40px;
14   }
```

%

The size of the margin as a percentage, relative to the inline size of the containing block.

```css
.box-1 {
    margin: 3%;
}
```

```
12   .box-1 {
13     margin: 3%;
14   }
```

auto

The browser selects a suitable margin to use. For example, in certain cases this value can be used to center an element.

You can set the margin property to auto to horizontally center the element within its container.

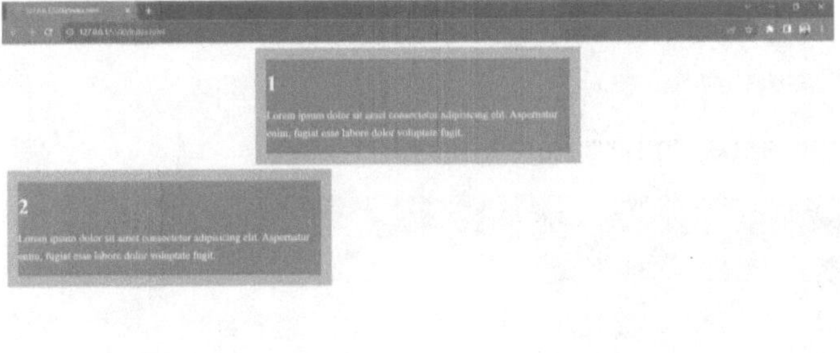

```
.box-1 {

    margin: 10px auto;

}
```

```
12    .box-1 {
13        margin: 10px auto;
14    }
```

The element will then take up the specified width, and the remaining space will be split equally between the left and right margins.

Shorthand values

It can accept

- one value for all sides
- two values for (top and bottom) (left and right)
- three values for (top) (right and left) (bottom)

- four values for (top) (right) (bottom) (left) - starting from top and moving in a clockwise direction.

margin accepts negative values

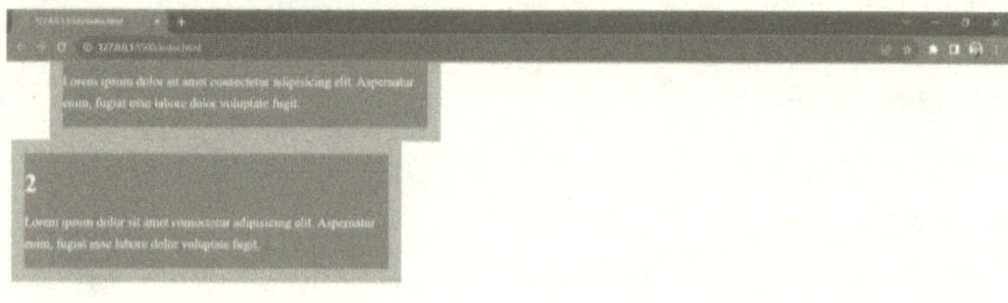

```
.box-1 {

    margin-left: 60px;

    margin-top: -100px;

}
```

```
12   .box-1 {
13     margin-left: 60px;
14     margin-top: -100px;
15   }
```

This can be useful when you want to overlap elements or adjust their positioning in unique ways.

padding

An element's padding is the space between its content and its border.

This property can have between one and four values:

- padding: <top> <right> <bottom> <left>
- padding: <top> <right and left> <bottom>
- padding: <top and bottom> <right and left>
- padding: <all sides>

Values

- length
- %

length

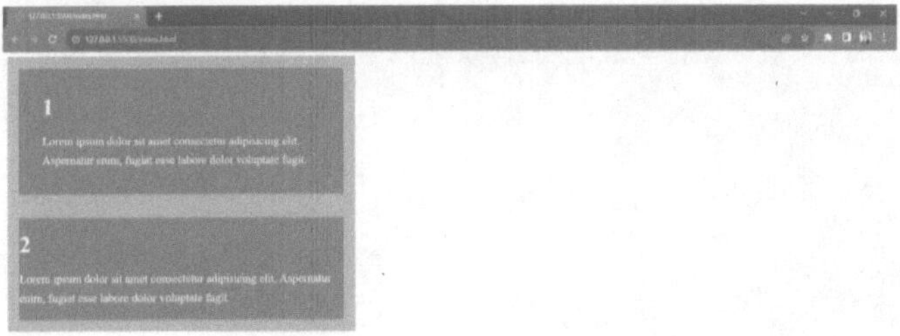

```
.box-1 {
    padding-top: 20px;
    padding-right: 40px;
```

```
        padding-bottom: 20px;

        padding-left: 40px;

    }
```

```
12   .box-1 {
13     padding-top: 20px;
14     padding-right: 40px;
15     padding-bottom: 20px;
16     padding-left: 40px;
17   }
```

You can use the shorthand property as follows

```
    .box-1 {

        padding-top: 20px 40px 20px 40px;

    }
```

```
12   .box-1 {
13     padding-top: 20px 40px 20px 40px;
14   }
```

%

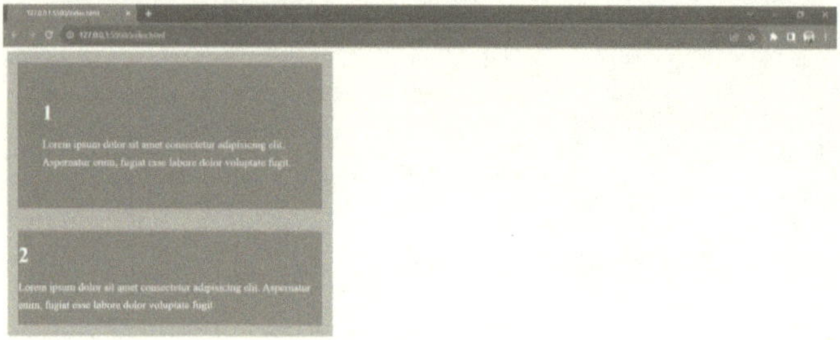

```
    .box-1 {

        padding: 3%;

    }
```

```
12   .box-1 {
13      padding: 3%;
14   }
```

auto

Specifying the keyword auto as a value has no effect on padding.

Shorthand values

It can accept

- one value for all sides
- two values for (top and bottom) (left and right)
- three values for (top) (right and left) (bottom)
- four values for (top) (right) (bottom) (left) - starting from top and moving in a clockwise direction.

Negative values

Using a negative number as a value has no effect on padding.

Margin Collapse

The upper and lower margins of elements are sometimes combined into a single margin, which corresponds to the largest of the two margins.

- This does not happen with left and right margins! Only at the top and bottom margins!

- In a container whose display is set to Flex or Grid, the margins don't collapse.

Example

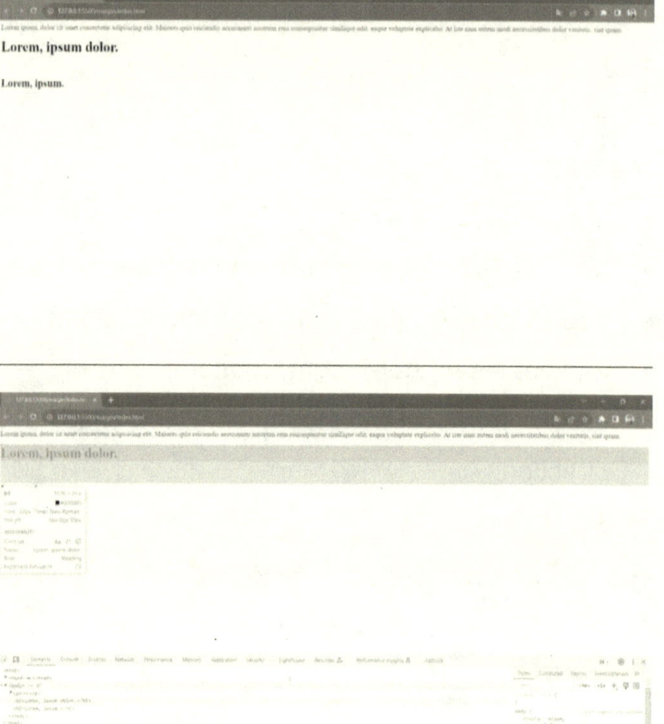

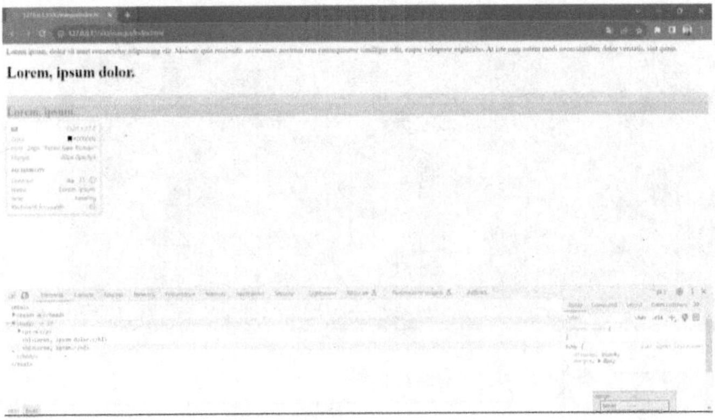

```html
<style>
  h1 {
    margin: 0 0 50px 0;
  }
  h2 {
    margin: 20px 0 0 0;
  }
</style>
<p>
  Lorem ipsum, dolor sit amet consectetur
adipisicing elit. Maiores quia
  reiciendis accusamus nostrum rem consequuntur
similique odit, eaque voluptate
  explicabo. At iste nam autem modi
necessitatibus dolor veritatis, sint quam.
</p>
<h1>Lorem, ipsum dolor.</h1>
```

```
<h2>Lorem, ipsum.</h2>
```

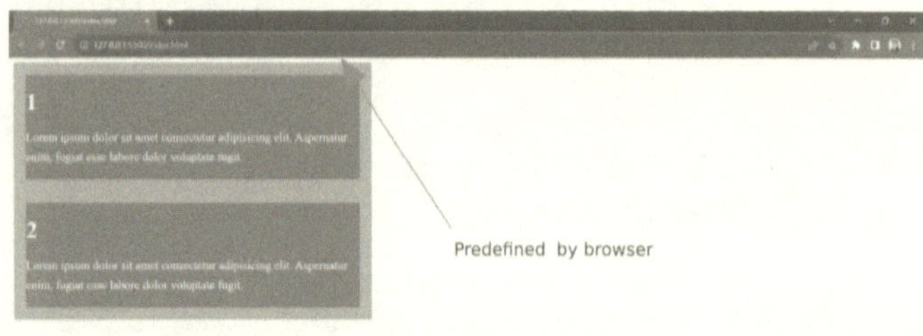

Universal selector reset

Browsers apply predefined styles to some HTML elements such as body, div, p, etc.

You can use the universal selector (*) to reset it as follows:

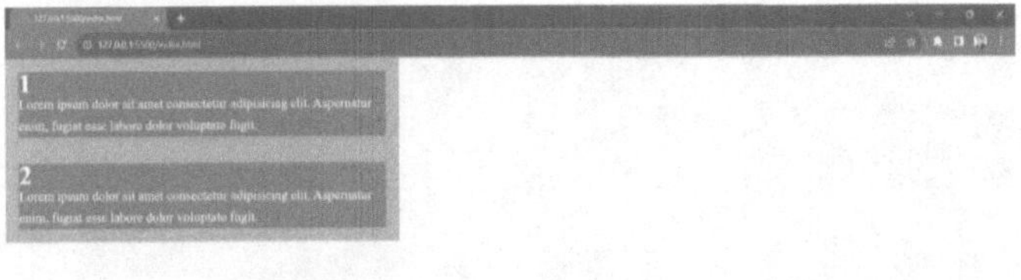

```css
* {
  margin: 0;
  padding: 0;
}
```

```css
2  * {
3    margin: 0;
4    padding: 0;
5  }
```

Put them at the beginning, because the styles are applied in order.

```html
<style>
  * {
    margin: 0;
    padding: 0;
  }
  .box {
    width: 600px;
    height: auto;
    color: white;
    font-size: 20px;
    line-height: 1.6em;
    background-color: rgb(0, 100, 128);
    border: 20px solid rgb(252, 49, 232);
    box-sizing: border-box;
  }
  .box-1 {
  }
  .box-2 {
  }
</style>
<div class="box box-1">
  <h1>1</h1>
  <p>
    Lorem ipsum dolor sit amet consectetur adipisicing elit. Aspernatur enim,
    fugiat esse labore dolor voluptate fugit.
  </p>
</div>
<div class="box box-2">
  <h1>2</h1>
  <p>
    Lorem ipsum dolor sit amet consectetur adipisicing elit. Aspernatur enim,
    fugiat esse labore dolor voluptate fugit.
  </p>
</div>
```

Chapter 4: Width and Height Properties

The width property sets the width of an element.

- The width of an element does not include padding, borders, or margins!
- The min-width and max-width properties override the width property.

Values

- auto (default)
- length
- %

auto (default)

The browser calculates the width

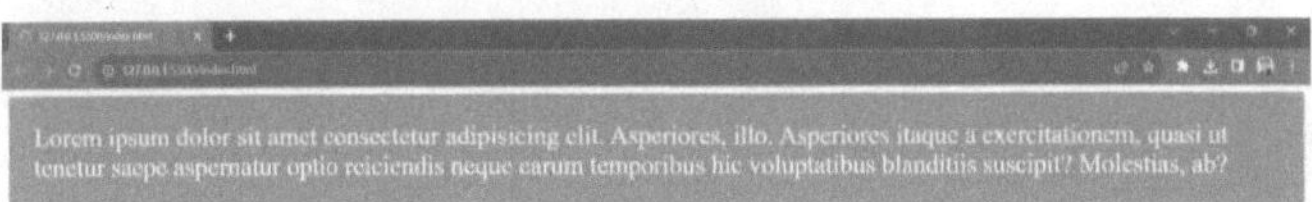

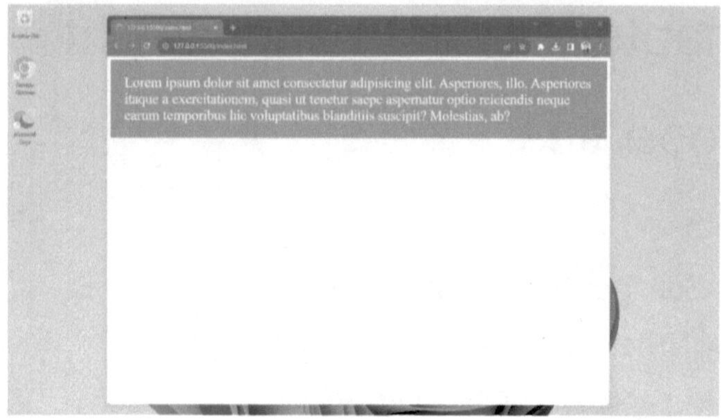

```html
<style>
  .div-1 {
    font-size: 30px;
    padding: 30px;
    color: white;
    background-color: royalblue;
    box-sizing: border-box;
    width: auto;
  }
</style>
<div class="div-1">
  Lorem ipsum dolor sit amet consectetur
  adipisicing elit. Asperiores, illo.
  Asperiores itaque a exercitationem, quasi ut
  tenetur saepe aspernatur optio
  reiciendis neque earum temporibus hic
  voluptatibus blanditiis suscipit?
```

        Molestias, ab?

</div>

```html
1   <style>
2     .div-1 {
3       font-size: 30px;
4       padding: 30px;
5       color: white;
6       background-color: royalblue;
7       box-sizing: border-box;
8       width: auto;
9     }
10  </style>
11  <div class="div-1">
12    Lorem ipsum dolor sit amet consectetur adipisicing elit. Asperiores, illo.
13    Asperiores itaque a exercitationem, quasi ut tenetur saepe aspernatur optio
14    reiciendis neque earum temporibus hic voluptatibus blanditiis suscipit?
15    Molestias, ab?
16  </div>
```

length

Defines the width in px, cm, etc.

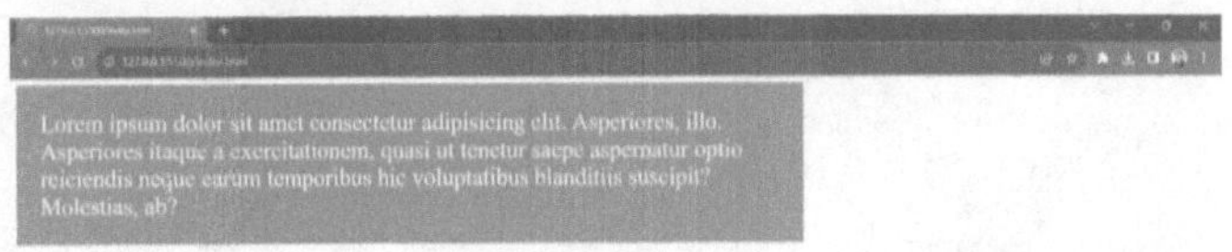

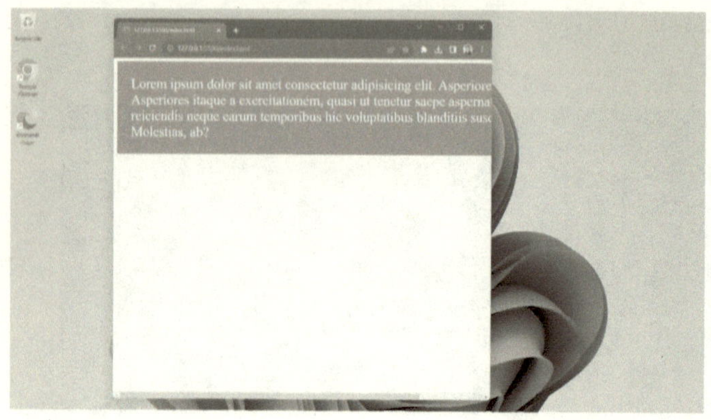

```css
.div-1 {

    font-size: 30px;

    padding: 30px;

    color: white;

    background-color: royalblue;

    box-sizing: border-box;

    width: 1000px;

}
```

%

Defines the width in percent of the containing block

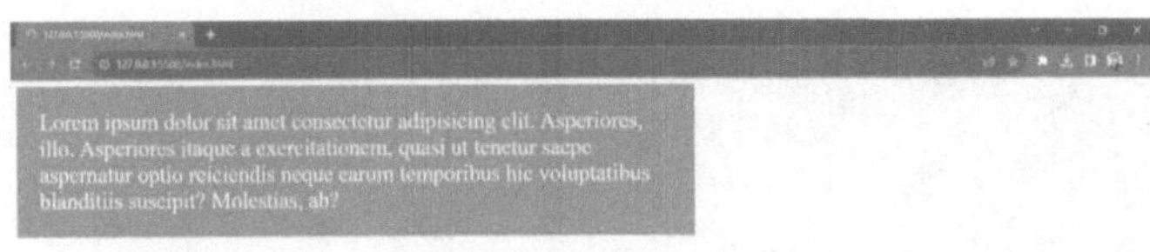

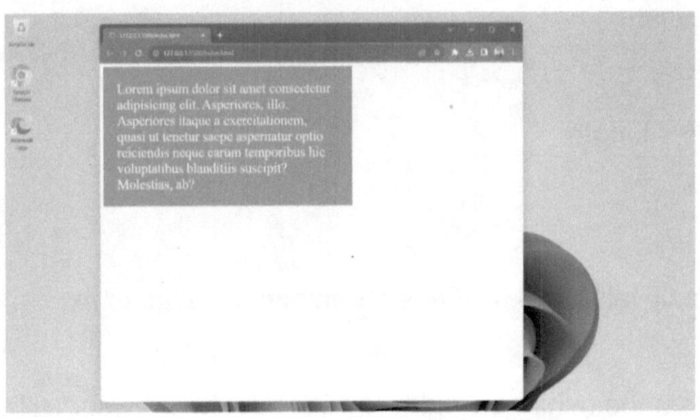

```css
.div-1 {
    font-size: 30px;
    padding: 30px;
    color: white;
    background-color: royalblue;
    box-sizing: border-box;
    width: 60%;
}
```

```css
2  .div-1 {
3    font-size: 30px;
4    padding: 30px;
5    color: white;
6    background-color: royalblue;
7    box-sizing: border-box;
8    width: 60%;
9  }
```

min-width

The CSS property min-width defines the minimum width of an element. It prevents the value used for the width property from being smaller than the value specified for min-width.

Values

- length
- %

length

Default value is 0. Defines the minimum width in px, cm, etc.

I've set the minimum width to 1000px. The browser still calculates the width, but it cannot be smaller than 1000 pixels.

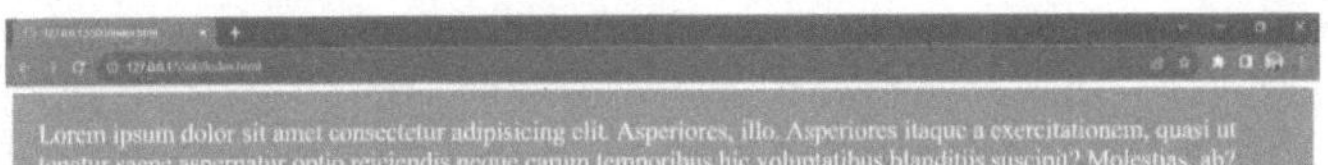

Lorem ipsum dolor sit amet consectetur adipisicing elit. Asperiores, illo. Asperiores itaque a exercitationem, quasi ut tenetur saepe aspernatur optio reiciendis neque earum temporibus hic voluptatibus blanditiis suscipit? Molestias, ab?

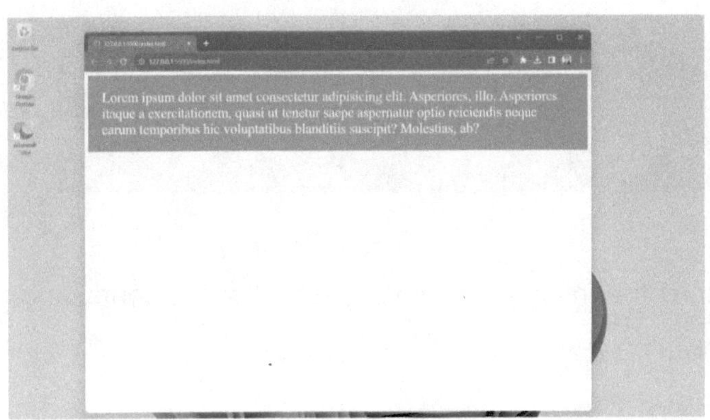

Lorem ipsum dolor sit amet consectetur adipisicing elit. Asperiores, illo. Asperiores itaque a exercitationem, quasi ut tenetur saepe aspernatur optio reiciendis neque earum temporibus hic voluptatibus blanditiis suscipit? Molestias, ab?

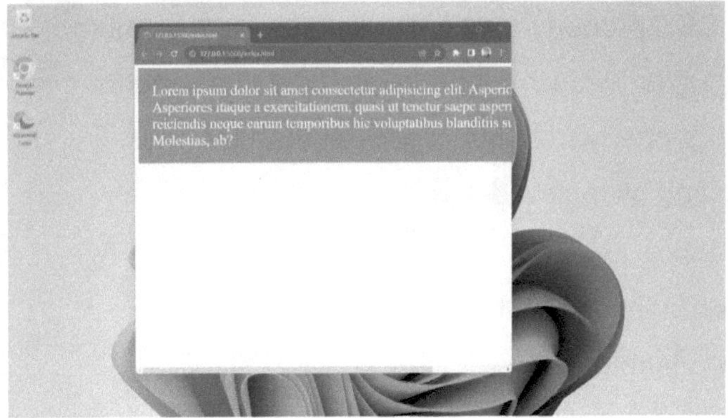

Lorem ipsum dolor sit amet consectetur adipisicing elit. Asperio Asperiores itaque a exercitationem, quasi ut tenetur saepe aspern reiciendis neque earum temporibus hic voluptatibus blanditiis su Molestias, ab?

```css
.div-1 {
    font-size: 30px;
    padding: 30px;
    color: white;
    background-color: royalblue;
    box-sizing: border-box;
    width: auto;
    min-width: 1000px;
}
```

```css
.div-1 {
    font-size: 30px;
    padding: 30px;
    color: white;
    background-color: royalblue;
    box-sizing: border-box;
    width: auto;
    min-width: 1000px;
}
```

%

Defines the minimum width in percent of the containing block

max-width

The CSS property max-width defines the maximum width of an element. It prevents the value used for the width property from being greater than the value specified by max-width.

Values

- none (default)
- length

- %

none (default)

No maximum width.

length

Defines the maximum width in px, cm, etc.

%

Defines the maximum width in percent of the containing block

I've set the maximum width to 50% of the container width. The browser still calculates the width, but it cannot be greater than 50%.

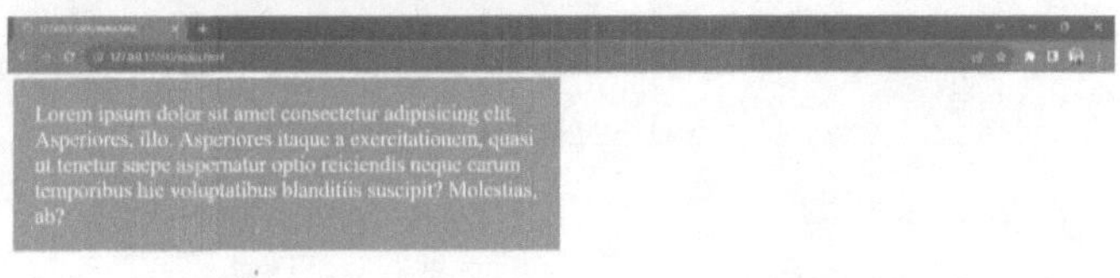

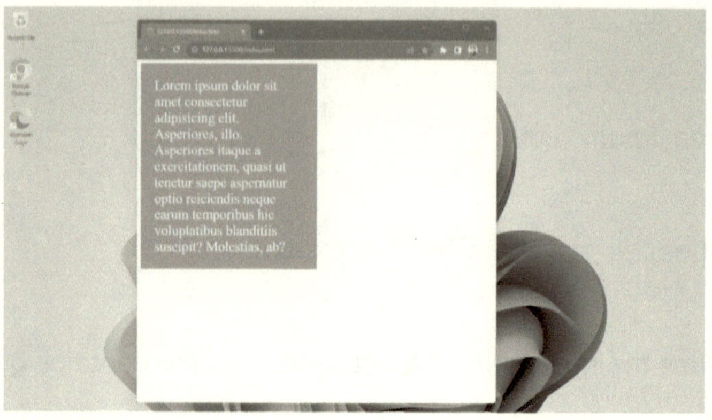

```css
.div-1 {
    font-size: 30px;
    padding: 30px;
    color: white;
    background-color: royalblue;
    box-sizing: border-box;
    width: auto;
    max-width: 50%;
}
```

height

The height CSS property specifies the height of an element.

- auto (default)
- length
- %

auto (default)

The browser calculates the height.

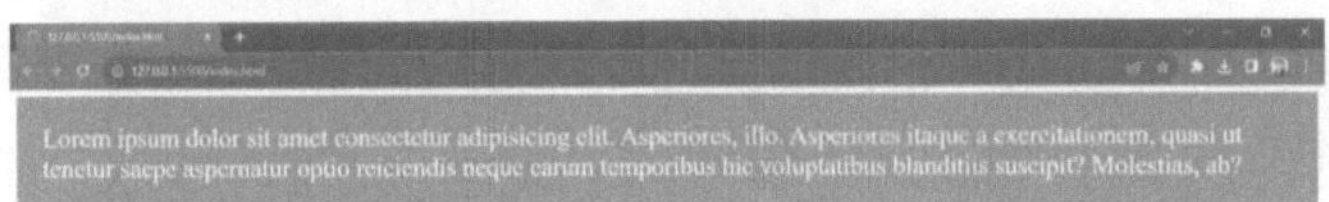

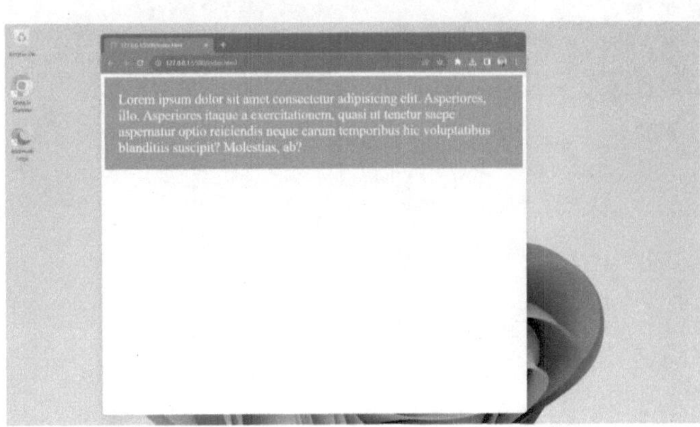

```
.div-1 {
    font-size: 30px;
```

```
    padding: 30px;

    color: white;

    background-color: royalblue;

    box-sizing: border-box;

    width: auto;

    height: auto;

}
```

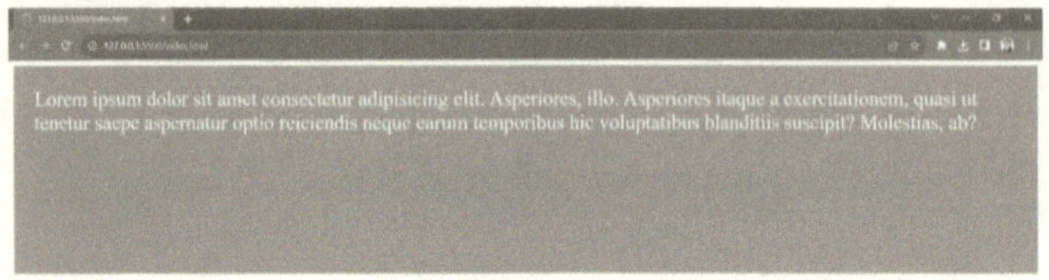

```
 2   .div-1 {
 3       font-size: 30px;
 4       padding: 30px;
 5       color: white;
 6       background-color: royalblue;
 7       box-sizing: border-box;
 8       width: auto;
 9       height: auto;
10   }
```

length

Defines the height in px, cm, etc.

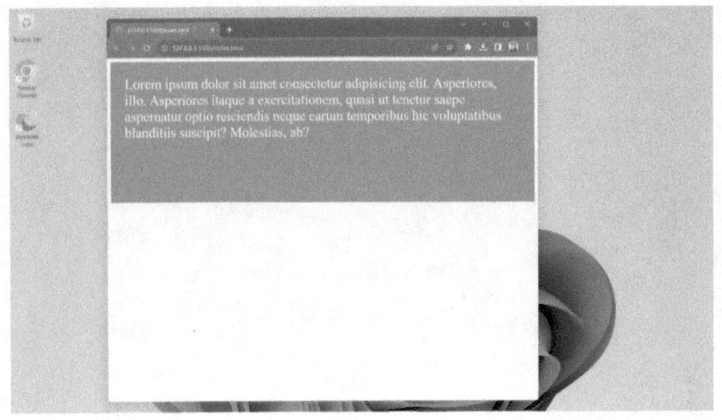


```css
.div-1 {
    font-size: 30px;
    padding: 30px;
    color: white;
    background-color: royalblue;
    box-sizing: border-box;
    width: auto;
    height: 300px;
}
```

```css
2   .div-1 {
3       font-size: 30px;
4       padding: 30px;
5       color: white;
6       background-color: royalblue;
7       box-sizing: border-box;
8       width: auto;
9       height: 300px;
10  }
```

%

Defines the height in percent of the containing block

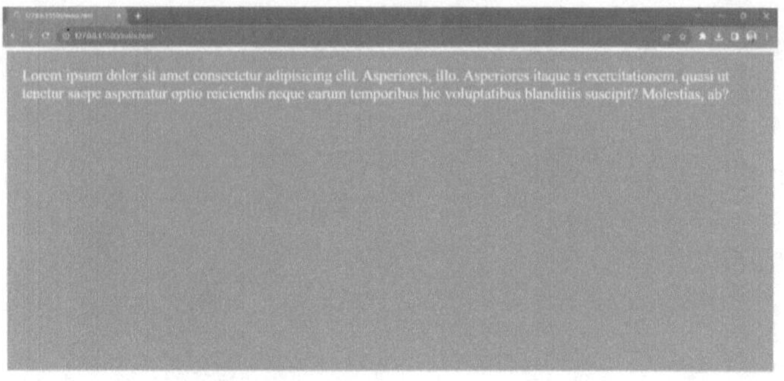

```css
.div-1 {
    font-size: 30px;
    padding: 30px;
    color: white;
    background-color: royalblue;
    box-sizing: border-box;
    width: auto;
    height: 80%;
}
```

```css
  .div-1 {
    font-size: 30px;
    padding: 30px;
    color: white;
    background-color: royalblue;
    box-sizing: border-box;
    width: auto;
    height: 80%;
  }
```

min-height

The CSS property min-height defines the minimum
height of an element. It prevents the value used for the
height property from being smaller than the value
specified for min-height.

Values

- length
- %

length

Default value is 0. Defines the minimum height in px,
cm, etc

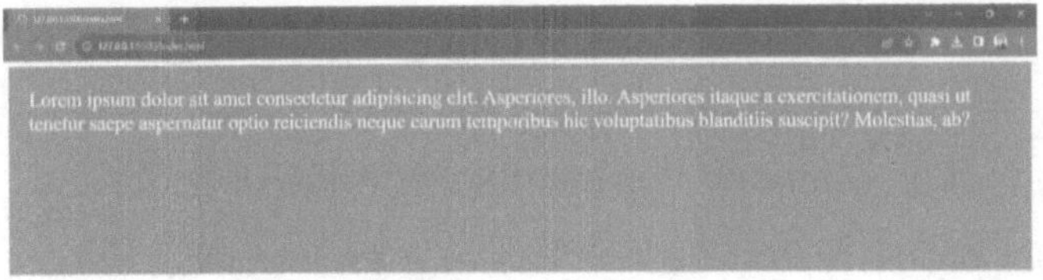

```css
.div-1 {
    font-size: 30px;
    padding: 30px;
    color: white;
    background-color: royalblue;
    box-sizing: border-box;
    width: auto;
    min-height: 300px;
}
```

```css
2   .div-1 {
3       font-size: 30px;
4       padding: 30px;
5       color: white;
6       background-color: royalblue;
7       box-sizing: border-box;
8       width: auto;
9       min-height: 300px;
10  }
```

%

Defines the minimum height in percent of the containing block

max-height

The CSS property max-height defines the maximum height of an element. It prevents the value used for the height property from being greater than the value specified for max-height.

Values

- none (default)
- length

- %

none (default)

No maximum height.

length

Defines the maximum height in px, cm, etc.

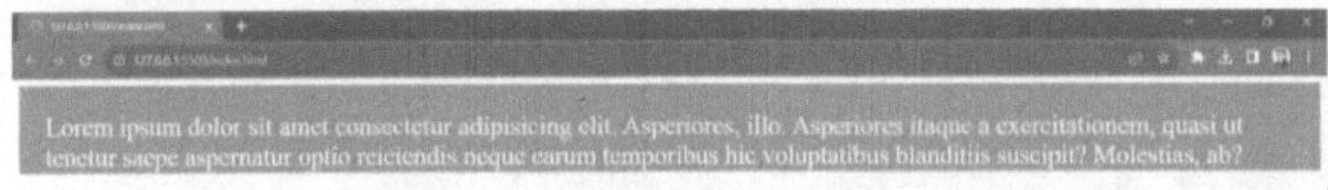

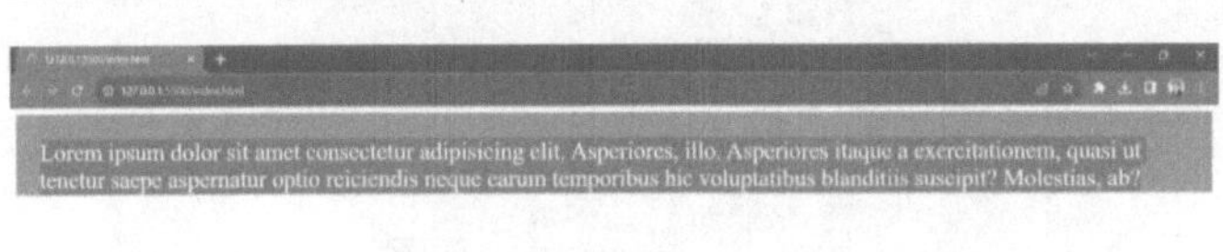

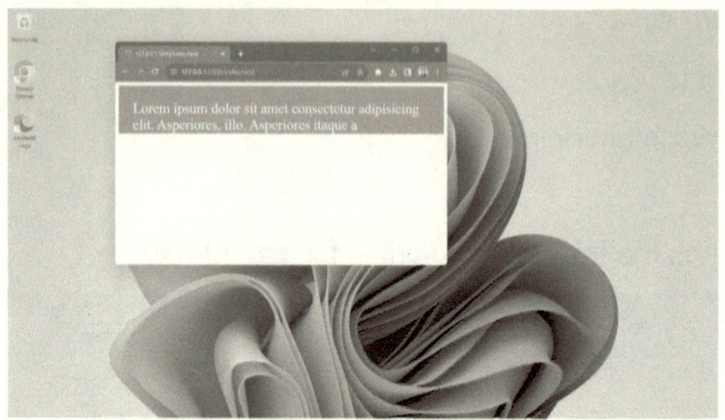

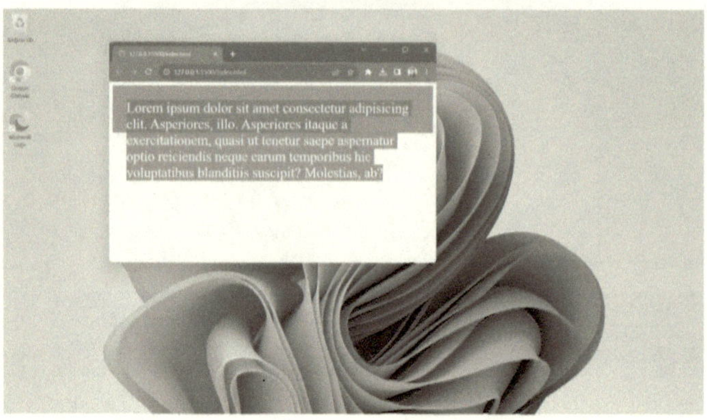

```css
.div-1 {
    font-size: 30px;
    padding: 30px;
    color: white;
    background-color: royalblue;
    box-sizing: border-box;
    width: auto;
    max-height: 100px;
}
```

```css
2   .div-1 {
3       font-size: 30px;
4       padding: 30px;
5       color: white;
6       background-color: royalblue;
7       box-sizing: border-box;
8       width: auto;
9       max-height: 100px;
10  }
```

%

Defines the maximum height in percent of the containing block.

If the content is larger than the maximum height, it will overflow. How the container will handle the overflowing content is defined by the overflow property.

overflow

The overflow property defines what should happen if the content exceeds the frame of an element.

This property determines whether the content should be cut off or scrollbars added if the content of an element is too large to fit in a certain area.

Values

- visible (default)
- hidden
- clip
- scroll
- auto

The overflow is not clipped. It renders outside the element's box.

```css
.div-1 {
    font-size: 30px;
    padding: 30px;
    color: white;
    background-color: royalblue;
    box-sizing: border-box;
    width: auto;
    max-height: 100px;
    overflow: visible;
}
```

```html
<style>
  .div-1 {
    width: 800px;
    max-height: 400px;
    background-color: lightblue;
    overflow: visible;
  }
</style>
<div class="div-1">
  <p>
    Lorem ipsum dolor sit amet consectetur adipisicing elit. Animi hic impedit
    beatae quisquam perspiciatis iusto, nemo eos nostrum aliquid debitis
    dolores, quos eligendi at commodi itaque esse placeat fugit excepturi,
    facilis unde possimus obcaecati. Commodi quam assumenda esse repellendus
    ullam.
  </p>
  <img src="image.jpg" />
</div>
```

hidden

The overflow is clipped, and the rest of the content will be invisible. Content can be scrolled programmatically (e.g. by setting scrollLeft or scrollTo())

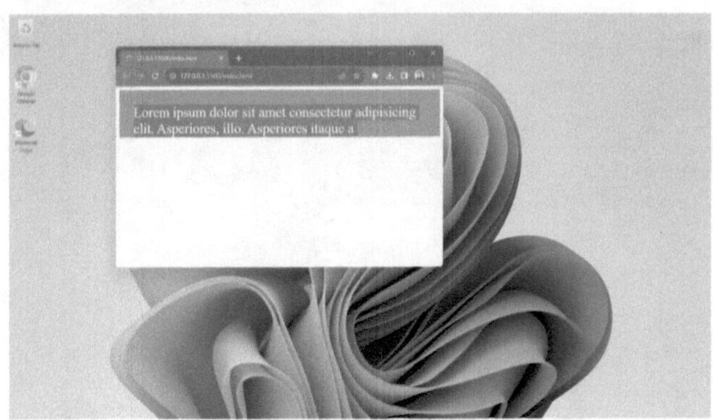


```css
.div-1 {
    font-size: 30px;
    padding: 30px;
    color: white;
    background-color: royalblue;
    box-sizing: border-box;
```

```
    width: auto;
    max-height: 100px;
    overflow: hidden;
}
```

```
2   .div-1 {
3     font-size: 30px;
4     padding: 30px;
5     color: white;
6     background-color: royalblue;
7     box-sizing: border-box;
8     width: auto;
9     max-height: 100px;
10    overflow: hidden;
11  }
```

clip

The overflow is clipped, and the rest of the content will be invisible. Forbids scrolling, including programmatic scrolling.

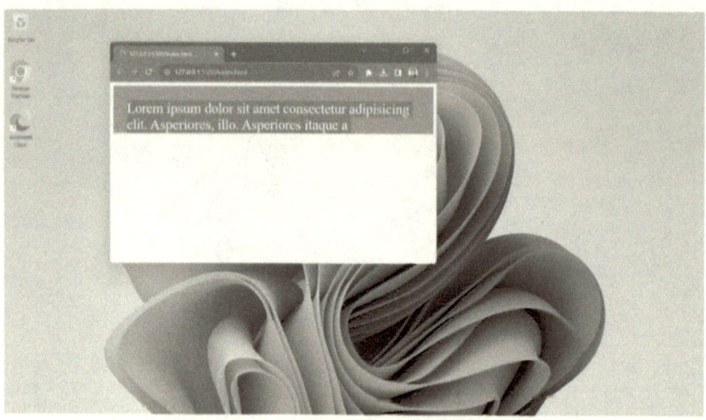


```
.div-1 {
    font-size: 30px;
    padding: 30px;
    color: white;
```

```css
    background-color: royalblue;
    box-sizing: border-box;
    width: auto;
    max-height: 100px;
    overflow: clip;
}
```

```css
 2    .div-1 {
 3        font-size: 30px;
 4        padding: 30px;
 5        color: white;
 6        background-color: royalblue;
 7        box-sizing: border-box;
 8        width: auto;
 9        max-height: 100px;
10        overflow: clip;
11    }
```

scroll

The overflow is clipped, but a scroll-bar is added to see the rest of the content

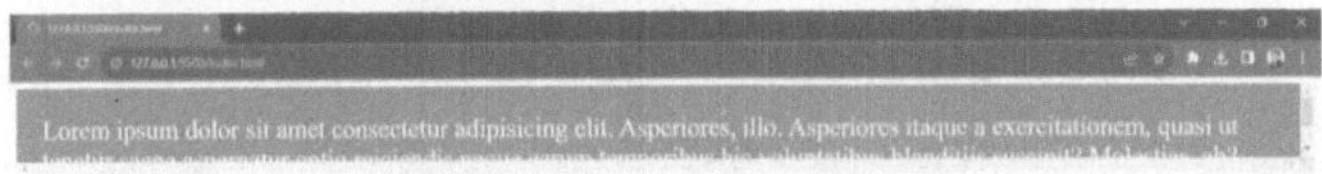

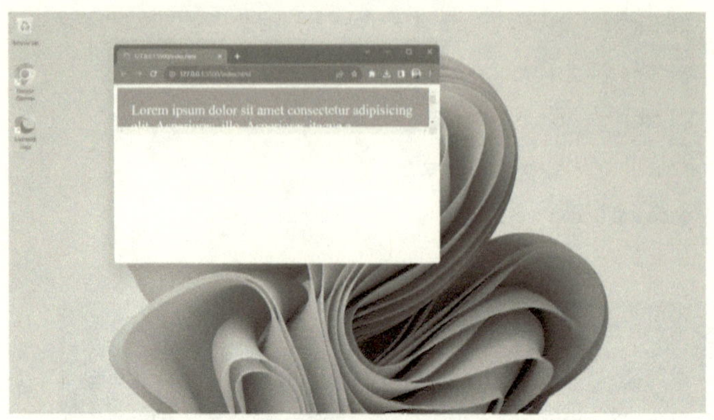

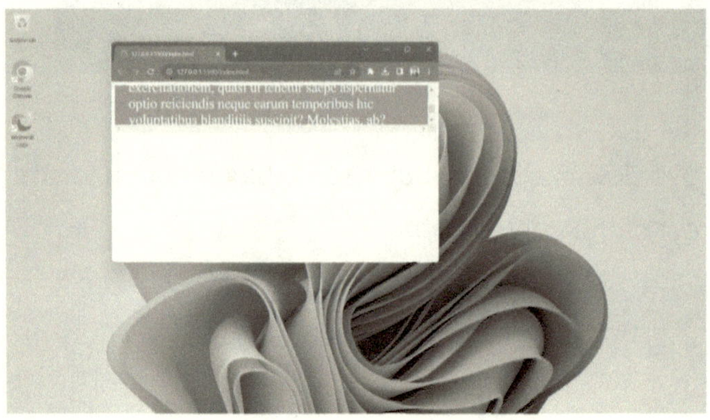

```css
.div-1 {
    font-size: 30px;
    padding: 30px;
    color: white;
    background-color: royalblue;
    box-sizing: border-box;
    width: auto;
    max-height: 100px;
    overflow: scroll;
```

```css
    }
  .div-1 {
    font-size: 30px;
    padding: 30px;
    color: white;
    background-color: royalblue;
    box-sizing: border-box;
    width: auto;
    max-height: 100px;
    overflow: scroll;
  }
```

auto

If overflow is clipped, a scroll-bar should be added to see the rest of the content

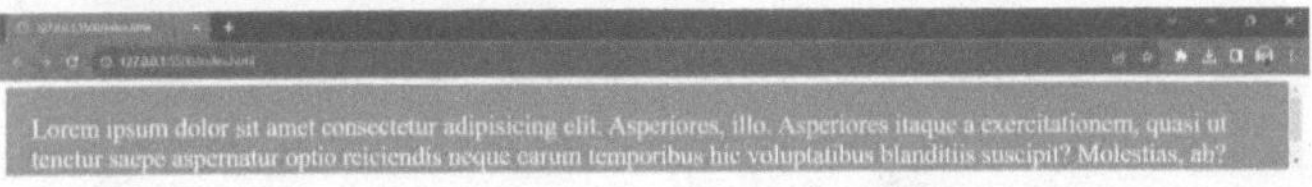

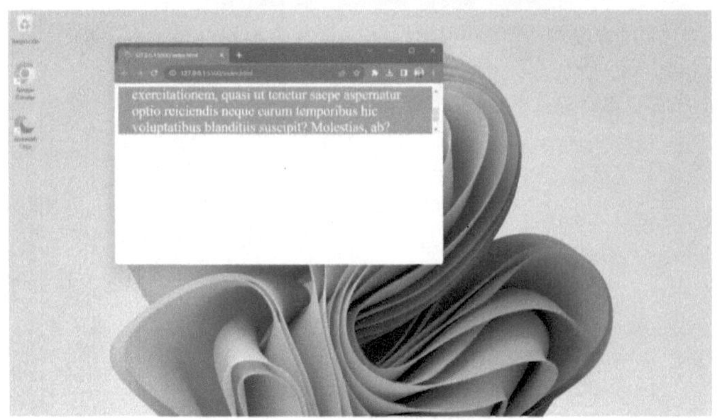


```css
.div-1 {
    font-size: 30px;
    padding: 30px;
    color: white;
    background-color: royalblue;
    box-sizing: border-box;
    width: auto;
    max-height: 100px;
    overflow: auto;
```

```css
}

 2   .div-1 {
 3       font-size: 30px;
 4       padding: 30px;
 5       color: white;
 6       background-color: royalblue;
 7       box-sizing: border-box;
 8       width: auto;
 9       max-height: 100px;
10       overflow: auto;
11   }
```

Only the vertical scroll bar has been added, as the horizontal bar is not needed.

overflow-x

The CSS property overflow-x defines what is displayed when the content overflows the left and right edges of a block-level element.

overflow-y

The CSS property overflow-y defines what is displayed when the content exceeds the top and bottom edges of a block-level element.

Conclusion

Congratulations! You have completed the book "CSS Box Model". Now you know everything about the CSS box model. Remember that learning CSS is an ongoing process. Practice makes perfect — create your own projects, experiment with the features you have learned, and take advantage of the extensive online resources. Thank you for joining me in my exploration of the CSS box model. I wish you the best of luck on your coding journey.

Good luck with your career and your personal brand and I will see you in other topics.

Media Attribution

Yellow empty frame on colorful background

Image by freepik

Don't miss out!

Receive an email when Abdelfattah Ragab publishes a new book. It's free and without obligation.

Also by Abdelfattah Ragab

About the Author

Abdelfattah Ragab is a professional software developer
with more than 20 years of experience.
https://abdelfattah-ragab.com

About the Publisher

Abdelfattah Ragab is a highly qualified and experienced software developer with over 20 years of experience in the industry. Specializing in front-end development, Abdelfattah Ragab has a deep understanding of Angular, JavaScript, TypeScript, HTML and CSS. Read more at https://abdelfattah-ragab.com

www.ingramcontent.com/pod-product-compliance
Lightning Source LLC
LaVergne TN
LVHW090220180726
843492LV00012B/2643